This edition published 2004 by
Mercury Books
20 Bloomsbury Street
London WC1B 3JH
ISBN 1-904668-68-2
Copyright © 2003 Allegra Publishing Ltd

Publisher: Felicia Law
Design director: Tracy Carrington
Project manager: Karen Foster
Author: Gerry Bailey
Editor: Rosalind Beckman
Designed by: Jacqueline Palmer
assisted by Fanny Level, Will Webster
Cartoon illustrations: Steve Boulter (Advocate)
and Andrew Keylock (Specs Art Agency)
Make-and-do: Jan Smith
Model-maker: Tim Draper
further models: Robert Harvey, Abby Dean
Photo studio: Steve Lumb
Photo research: Diana Morris
Scanning: Acumen Colour
Proof-reading: Victoria Grimsell
Digital workflow: Edward MacDermott

Printed by D 2 Print Singapore

Crafty Inventions

LONG LONG AGO

Contents

Mercury Junior

20 BLOOMSBURY STREET
LONDON WC1B 3JH

What can I use to hunt the lion?

Belo the hunter is hungry. He needs to go out hunting, except there is nothing around to hunt. Everything has been chased away by a lion. Belo has to do something about the lion, but how can he hunt and kill such a dangerous beast?

Belo looks at his hunting equipment - a few stones and a small stick he throws at animals. He is used to driving some animals over cliffs as well. But there are no animals to chase.

> I'm so hungry. How can I catch some food without the lion catching me?

The lion is a dangerous beast. How can Belo get close enough to throw a rock at it? And he dare not miss. Perhaps he could sharpen his stick. But then he'd have to get even closer.

WHAT CAN HE DO?

- Dress up and paint his face, then try to frighten the lion away. But lions aren't afraid of much.

- Dig a pit and lure the lion into it with some bait. But he has no bait - except himself. That's no good.

- Sharpen his stick and get close enough to throw it. Pretty dangerous. And would the stick be sharp enough, anyway?

- What if he used his flint knife to throw at the lion? That's a good idea because it's sharp. But it won't fly through the air easily.

I'll put the two ideas together to make a throwing blade called a spear. I'll cut a notch at one end of my stick and fit the flint blade into the notch. I'll bind it tightly with grass twine. Now I can hunt the lion from a safe distance.

Later, spear heads like these were made of bronze.

Spearheads

In prehistoric times people made **spears** and arrowheads from sharpened **flint** stones. The flint head was bound to a long wooden pole, or shaft, with cord. The spear could be thrown a great distance because of its **aerodynamic** shape. Hunters used their spears to hunt wild animals.

These included large cats, wild boar, reindeer, bison and elk. Spear-throwing became a skill the hunter had to master at a young age. Later, spears were used in battle, for both attack and defence. A soldier holding a spear could keep an enemy at more than an arm's length away.

Aerodynamics

Aerodynamics is the study of the forces that act on an object as it moves through the air. It is important to designers and engineers working on moving things such as aeroplanes, rockets and cars.

When an object moves through air, the air rubs against it. This rubbing, called **friction**, slows the object down. Scientists and engineers try to overcome friction by designing objects that rub as little as possible on the air. An object that reduces friction in this way is called aerodynamic.

An aeroplane is very aerodynamic. Its sharp, pointed nose allows it to cut through the atmosphere easily. The nose of the plane pushes the air aside so friction is reduced. The smooth metal surface of the plane makes sure that friction is reduced even more.

RACING CARS

The first racing cars were not very aerodynamic. They were too bulky at the front. Today's racing cars use aerodynamics to create smooth shapes that cut through the air. To achieve the best shape possible, racing cars are sent to special wind tunnels **for testing.**

Inventor's words

aerodynamic
friction
flint
spear
wind tunnel

This aeroplane has an aerodynamic shape. The front is wedge-shaped to reduce friction. The sides are smooth, which also reduces friction.

Make your own aerodynamic spears

You will need

• paper • scissors
• glue
• paint

1 Cut a thin strip of paper about 4cm wide.

2 Take a piece of paper about 20cm x 10cm and fold it in half to make a square. Glue the thin strip to the inside so the long tail sticks out.

3 Fold the square to make a paper dart (the spearhead), with the thin strip as the spear handle inside. Glue together.

4 Paint and decorate your collection of aerodynamic spears and darts.

5 You can experiment with different shapes of dart and different lengths of tail to find out which designs fly best. Try adding a paper clip to the nose to balance the flight.

Which aerodynamic design flies best?

How can I pull a heavy sled?

Indo is a hunter. He drags a sled with him on the hunt so he can bring the animals back home. But today is different. He has fallen and injured his leg. It is too dangerous to leave him as there are wild animals around. Lea, his wife, must put Indo on the sled and pull him home instead.

> The sled is impossible to push. What can I use to help move my heavy husband?

Lea tries to push the sled. But with Indo on top, it's just too heavy and it won't budge.

WHAT CAN SHE DO?

- Tell Indo to hop home as fast as he can and hope the wild animals are slower and better fed than he is. A fat chance!

- How about raiding a bee hive for the honey, then spreading a slippery path and sliding Indo home? But she'd be stung!!

- Roll the sled home over some logs. She'd need quite a few, though. But rolling sounds good.

- What if she used some short pieces of log instead of large, heavy ones, to move the sled along?

I'll chop narrow discs from the logs, because discs will roll along the ground. If I attach them under the sled, one at each corner, they'll move both the sled and the load. Then I'll fix the discs so they can spin round easily on a short pole.

A Chinese horse-cart with solid wheels.

Early wheels

A **wheel** is a round **disc**. It spins, or rotates, around a pole called an **axle**, which is fixed through the centre point of the disc. The idea of the wheel probably developed from the use of rolling logs to carry loads. As the load moved forward, the back log would be rushed to the front.

Progress was very slow. When disc-shaped wheels were fixed to a platform under the load, a huge leap forward in the history of transport was made. These wheels were heavy but they cut down even more on **friction**. This made pulling a load much easier for man and beast.

Friction

It is hard work dragging a heavy object such as a sled. The sled rubs against the rough surface of the ground underneath. This rubbing is caused by a force called friction. Friction is produced when two objects touch or rub against each other.

Friction is a force that tries to slow moving things down. It also tries to stop still things from starting to move in the first place. Any object that is moving or beginning to move will feel friction. But there is less friction between smooth surfaces than between rough surfaces. Skates, for example, glide easily over smooth ice, while the textured tread on tyres grip rough roads.

An Alaskan sled can carry a heavy load because the runners glide over smooth snow, which reduces the friction.

RUBBING TOGETHER

When two surfaces are pressed together, some of the atoms in each surface mix together, or 'weld'. When we try to move the two surfaces against each other, we have to break those 'welds'. The force that tries to stop us doing this is called friction.

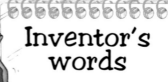

Inventor's words

atom • axle
disc
friction
wheel

Make a model cart

You will need

- a small box or food tub about 15cm x 7cm
- 2 small round foil baking cases
- sticky tape • 2 drawing pins
- 2 small pieces of cork or polystyrene packaging
- a small stick or wooden skewer
- string or twine
- paint and paintbrush

1 Cut the box down to make a shallow container and decorate it with paints.

2 Make the wheels by flattening the baking cases and sticking tape on one side to reinforce the centre. Alternatively, you could cut out wheels from a piece of cardboard.

3 Pin the wheels to the cart with the drawing pins on the outside and the cork on the inside.

4 Push a length of skewer into the base of the box and secure with tape. Tie a shorter stick on to make a crossbar.

You can add a piece of card to make a floor inside, if you like. Load your wagon with straw or raffia.

How can I lift the huge stones?

The ancient priest Corpulent is puzzled. He and his men have dragged huge stones called megaliths over many kilometres. Now they are lodged upright in the ground. But the men don't know how to finish the monument. They cannot raise the huge stones that go on top.

Corpulent wants to build a monument that's bigger and better than any seen before. He will lay stones called lintels on top of the megaliths.

But the stones are huge and incredibly heavy. No one has got the muscle to perform this mammoth task.

How can I raise the heavy lintels and place them securely across the top of the megaliths?

WHAT CAN HE DO?

- Make wooden blocks and paint them to look like rock, and hope the high priest won't notice.

- What if he hauled the lintels into place using ropes? Pulling with ropes might work if his men can take the strain.

- He could use as many men as possible to make a human slope or ramp. Good idea, but what about his men? They'd be crushed!

- Slide the lintels up a wooden ramp? Hmm! But it might work if the ramp is strong enough.

I'm sure the ramp will work, but it'll have to be strong, so I'm going to build one made of tightly-packed earth. Then I can pull the lintels up the earth ramp and slide them into place on top of the standing stones.

Scientists believe that earth ramps were used in the building of Stonehenge in Britain over 3500 years ago.

Earth ramp

An earth **ramp** is a solid, sloping surface made of earth, or rocks and earth tightly packed together. Since it is solid and therefore very sturdy, it can support very heavy weights. Earth ramps were used to help build many ancient buildings and **monuments**.

The ancient Egyptians built earth ramps to raise the huge blocks of stone that formed the pyramids. Early engineers used smaller earth ramps to haul **lintel** stones and ease them into place across two standing stones, called **megaliths**.

Ramps

A ramp is a sloping surface linking two places that are at different levels. A ramp is also known as an inclined plane.

Imagine a heavy barrel that needs to be lifted up to a high rack. You might be able lift the barrel straight up if you were very strong. But this would be hard work. Your muscle power would have to match the barrel's weight, or **load**.

Instead, you could roll the barrel up a ramp. Using a ramp is easier, because the weight of the force needed is much less than the load. The barrel may need to be pushed a longer distance, but because the load is lighter, pushing it a bit further is well worth it.

SKATEBOARD

Skateboarders sometimes use a ramp to give them more speed. The ramp works to reduce the upward force of the ground beneath. This allows gravity to pull skateboarders down along the ramp. The steeper the ramp the faster they are pulled down.

Inventor's words

gravity
inclined plane
lintel • load
megalith
monument
ramp

A ramp helps a wheelchair user to reach the same level as a person using steps.

Make a working force-measurer

You will need

- shelfboard, about 50–70cm long
- pencil • ruler
- drinking straw
- rubber band
- thin skewer or straightened wire coat hanger
- cocktail stick • drawing pin
- small toy truck, filled with sand or gravel
- string

1 Mark a scale on the shelfboard using a pencil and ruler.

2 Cut a length of drinking straw about 3cm long. Push the rubber band through it, using the skewer or wire hanger.

3 Make a pinhole through the straw, then push the cocktail stick through so it holds one end of the rubber band. Fix the other end of the rubber band to the board with the drawing pin.

4 Attach a string loop to the front of the truck, then hook this on to the cocktail stick.

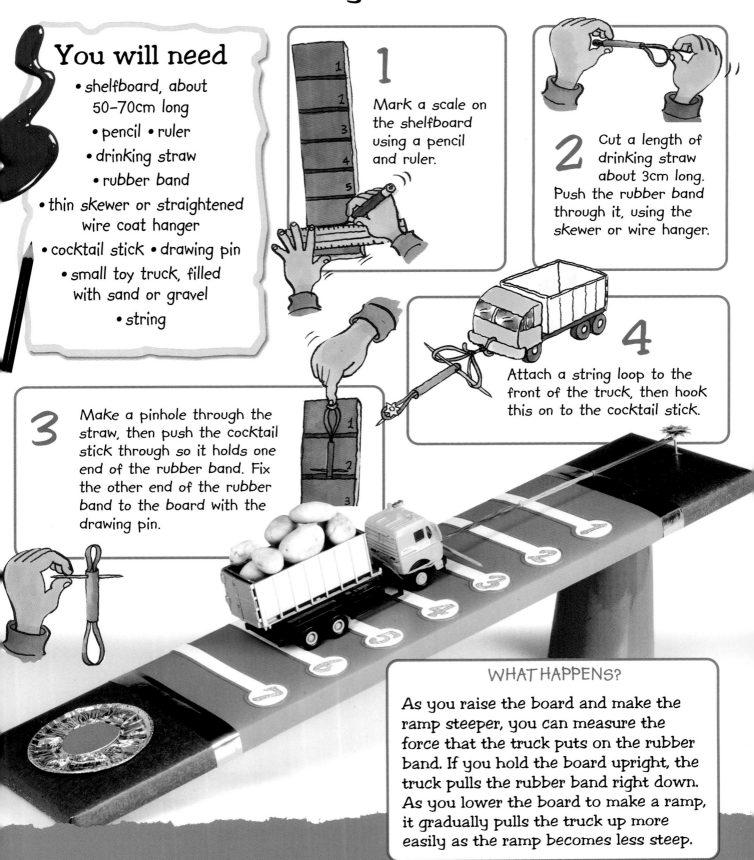

WHAT HAPPENS?

As you raise the board and make the ramp steeper, you can measure the force that the truck puts on the rubber band. If you hold the board upright, the truck pulls the rubber band right down. As you lower the board to make a ramp, it gradually pulls the truck up more easily as the ramp becomes less steep.

How can I plant my seeds?

Farmer Ham has a big field to plant and a lot of seeds to sow. But the earth in the field is hard and the seeds just lie on the surface when he throws them down. He needs to get the seeds into the rich earth if they are to grow well.

First, Ham uses a pointed stick to make holes in the ground into which he can drop the seeds. But it takes far too long and is tiring. The field is just too big.

Then Ham tries to stamp the seeds into the ground. But the earth is too hard and the seeds split or roll away. Some are stolen by the crows that watch and wait for easy pickings.

WHAT CAN HE DO?

- Ask the crows to help him. They can use their beaks to peck holes in the ground. But they'd probably eat most of the seed while they were at it!

- Scratching furrows with his fingers might work. The rows would be nice and straight, but not very deep. And his fingers would ache.

- What if he used a flat stick to scrape out a furrow in the ground? But sticks would soon become blunt or snap against the hard earth.

- An axe might be better. The furrows would be deeper, which is good, but it would be back-breaking work!

How can I plant my seeds deep enough to get the better of those pesky crows?

16

I've got a brilliant idea! I'll tie a large cutting blade behind my ox and use it to carve out a deep, straight furrow. I'll make sure that the ditch is the same depth all along its length. Then, as I walk behind the ox, I'll scatter seeds into the furrows.

A plough pulled by a water buffalo cuts into a watery paddy field in China.

The first plough

A **plough** is a machine that prepares land ready for seeds to be sown. It has a handle for steering and **blade** that acts as a **wedge**. The blade digs into the soil, loosening it and turning it over. Modern ploughs often have many rows of steel blades and are usually pulled by large tractors.

The first ploughs were probably used in China and parts of the Middle East. They were pulled by oxen and cut grooves called **furrows** into the soil. Similar horse-drawn ploughs are still used today. The farmer guides the plough with a handle to ensure that the furrows are straight.

The wedge

A wedge is a simple machine. It is used to push and spread things apart.

The blade of an **axe** is a type of wedge. When the cutting edge is driven into a log, the powerful movement creates a strong force that splits open the wood. The downward effort of the hand is changed into a sideways splitting effort that cuts the log.

SCISSOR BLADES

Most of the machines we use are made up of combinations of simple devices. An everyday example is the scissors. Each blade of the scissors is a wedge. But the two blades, or wedges, are joined to make another device - a **lever** - which gives the scissors an even stronger cutting action.

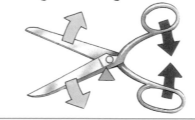

Any sharp object is a type of wedge – knives, arrows or needles are all wedges. The sharp **bow** of a ship acts as a wedge when it moves through the water. The pointed end of a rocket cuts through the air as it powers through the atmosphere.

A Vietnamese woman chopping wood.

Inventor's words

axe • blade • bow
furrow • lever
plough • wedge

Make a traditional plough

You will need

- marker pen • scissors
- acrylic paint
- empty square-shaped plastic container, like a drink or household cleaner bottle
- strong glue to stick plastic
- forked twig (like the one in the picture) and some small straight twigs
- different kinds of string, or thin strips of leather or plastic

1 Draw the shape of the plough blade with a marker pen around the corner of the plastic container.

2 Cut out carefully with scissors. Then do exactly the same on the other side of the container. Now glue the two blades together.

3 Tie the plough blade to the twig so that the pointed curve will dig into the soil. Wind the string round and round to make it secure.

4 Make the plough handle by tying a short twig across the end of the plough. Tie another twig at the other end. Attach string or pieces of leather for the ropes to pull the plough.

5 Paint the blade of the plough with acrylic paint.

Push your plough through a tray of sand to make a furrow

How can I get water to my crops?

The River Nile runs through a hot, dry country called Egypt. Each year, the waters of the Nile rise up over its banks to flood the dry land on either side. The water helps the crops grow. But this year the Nile is very low. The water cannot reach the crops.

The waters of the Nile are not rising as usual this year. The soil in Farmer Gamel's field is dry and dusty.

The ditches that carry water through the fields are almost dry. The farmer's crops need water or they will soon wither and die.

> How can I get the water up the steep bank to my plants before they die?

Farmer Gamel is worried. The bank is too steep to haul up water.

WHAT CAN HE DO?

- Wait for it to rain. Hmm!

- Slide down the bank and fill his cupped hands with water. Then clamber back up to the dry plants. Exhausting!

- Tie a bucket to some rope, lower it into the water and pull it up full. A bucket's a good idea . . .

- Train an elephant to suck up water in its trunk, swing round and spray the crops. Yes, swinging could work . . .

- Tie a bucket to a plank. Dip the plank into the water and then bring it back up.

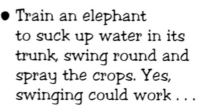

20

I know, I'll use a bucket and the swing idea, and make a water-dipper. I'll make a big lever with a bucket tied to a rope on one end and a weight on the other. And I'll call my gadget a shadoof.

The shadoof is still put to use in parts of Africa and India.

The shadoof

A **shadoof** is a water-raising device first used by the early Egyptians over 2000 years ago. It consists of a bucket-like container made from animal skins or clay that is tied to one end of a **lever**.

The other end of the lever is weighted with heavy stones. The container is dipped into the water. When full, it is lifted up and poured into ditches that carry water to **irrigate** the fields.

Levers

The lever is a simple machine that helps us do many different kinds of work. It is very useful, for example, when we need to lift something that is very heavy.

The most common kind of lever is a straight length of wood, such as a plank, that rests or balances on something underneath. The plank is called the **arm** and the place where it rests is called the **fulcrum**. Every lever has an arm and a fulcrum.

When you place a **load** on one end of the plank, you can lift it more easily by pushing down on the other end of the plank. The end of the plank, or arm, that you move is called the **force** or **effort** end. This is because you use force or effort to move it. The other end is called the load end because it carries the load that has to be moved.

CLAW HAMMER

A claw hammer is a simple lever that can yank a nail out of a piece of wood. The lower end of the claw hammer acts as the fulcrum. If you pull down the hammer at the upper end, a strong force raises the nail.

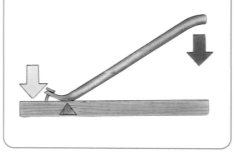

A seesaw is a type of lever. The fulcrum is the wooden stand in the centre. The arm carries the children.

Inventor's words

arm
effort
force • fulcrum
irrigate
lever • load
shadoof

Make a working shadoof

You will need

- 3 sticks, about 30 cms long
- tray of sand
- 1 shorter and 1 longer stick
- cocktail stick
- plastic cup
- string
- small pebbles

1 Tie the three 30cm sticks together and stand them in the tray of soil or gravel. Tie a small twig near the top as a rest for the beam.

2 Make the water container by pushing a cocktail stick through the plastic cup, and attaching string loops.

3 Loosely tie the long twig on to the beam-rest. Tie the cup to one end.

4 Bind a couple of pebbles together with string and tie them to the other end of the beam.

You can lower your shadoof over the kitchen sink and use it to raise water.

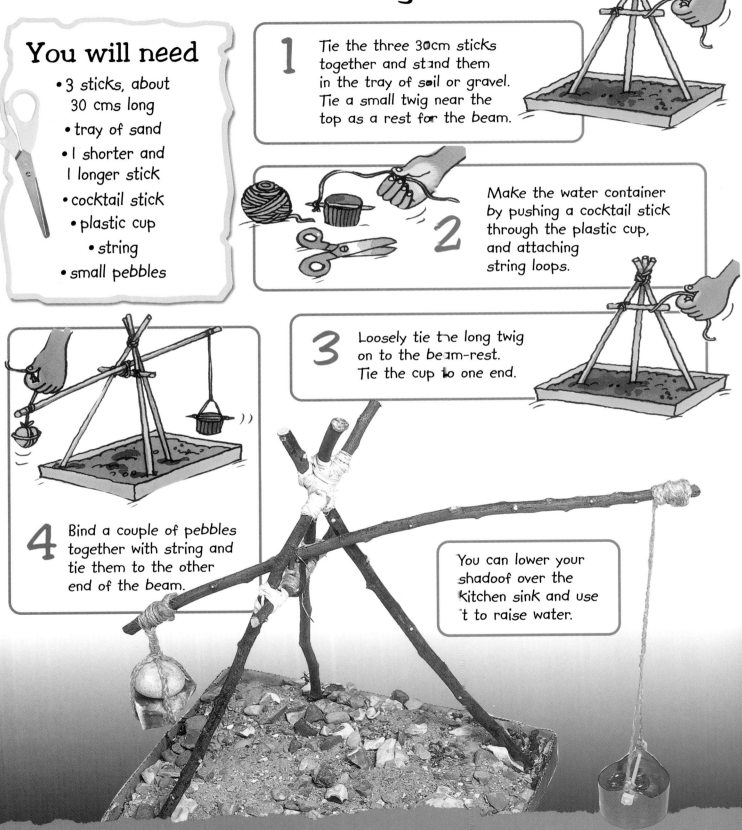

How fast can your shadoof raise water from the kitchen sink?

How can we travel on water?

In prehistoric times, the only way to go from one place to another was to walk or run. This was fine on land. But it was no good if you wanted to cross a river that was fast and deep - especially if you had a heavy load to carry!

Lem and his friends are looking for animals to hunt. Ahead is a deep, wide river. On the far side, a large herd of deer is grazing among the trees. How can the hunters get to the other side?

Even if I get across on a log, how can I bring a deer back?

WHAT CAN THEY DO?

- Brave the strong currents and swim across. But then they need to haul the dead animal back. Not easy!

- What if they each cut down a tree and paddle it across the river? After the hunt, they could tow the dead animal behind them. But the deer might sink.

- How about holding on to each other, and holding on to the logs, and holding on to the deer? How many hands is that . . ?

- They could use ropes of animal skin to tie themselves to the logs, or the deer to the logs - or just the logs to the logs . . .

Logs will be useful. We'll cut down some trees and tie the trunks together to make a platform. Then we'll be able to cross the river together, hunt for food and bring it back on this raft.

A log raft with special fencing is used to carry cattle across a river.

Log raft

The first **rafts** were probably just logs tied together with ropes made of animal skin. Two logs were used as **crossbeams** to **stabilise** the raft at each end. Sometimes, animal skins were **inflated** with air and attached under the raft to make it it more stable.

A stable raft can carry more people or goods. Rafts or flat boats such as these traded along the rivers of the world. In Egypt, long reeds were cut into bundles and fastened together. Later, the reed rafts were shaped and curved. These were the first boats.

Floating

All objects will either float or sink when placed in water. This will depend on both their weight and their size. The combination of the weight and size of an object is called density. Density means how much a certain amount, or volume, of material weighs.

Like all substances, water has density, too. An object that is less dense than the weight of the same amount of water will float. If the object is more dense than the same amount of water, it will sink. A pebble is made up of very dense material, packed tightly together. Although it is small, it will sink. It weighs far more than the weight of the same, tiny amount of water. It could never float!

A heavy dugout tree trunk will float, even with someone on it, because it is less dense than the water it is floating in.

DISPLACING WATER

A ship floats half in and half out of the water. It is less heavy than the water it has displaced. However, if the ship is loaded with extra goods, it will sink lower and lower. If it becomes heavier than the water it has displaced, the ship will sink.

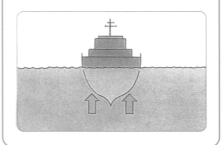

Inventor's words

crossbeam
density • displace
float • inflate
raft • stabilise
substance
volume

Craft a raft!

You will need

- several sticks or twigs cut to the same length
- string or garden raffia
- scissors
- bowl of water or large shallow dish

1 Line up the sticks so that they form a platform.

2 Use the string to lash the twigs together. The string should go over and under each stick in turn.

3 Now lash together the twigs at the other end in the same way. Take two twigs for the crossbars and trim to size.

4 Attach the crossbars to each end of the platform. Thread the string through the holes between the sticks and secure firmly.

5 Make different items of cargo to carry on the raft.
- A small piece of cloth tied around gravel makes a sack.
- Roll up fabric and tie in a bundle.
- Make a tub full of goods.
- Paint corks to look like barrels. Glue them to stack together.

How much cargo can your raft carry and still stay afloat? **27**

How can I cross the river?

Lamka the shepherdess needs to move her flock to a new pasture. But the grassy field lies across a wide, fast-moving stream. Lamka must think up a plan to get to the other side. Would that piece of old wood be of any use?

The piece of wood stretches across the river. The first sheep crosses safely. But the next few sheep to cross make the wood bend in the middle.

> How can I make it safe for my sheep to cross the stream to graze?

Lamka decides not to send over any more sheep. She imagines the wood bending so much that it cracks with the weight, carrying her flock into the stream.

WHAT CAN SHE DO?

- She could carry her sheep across one by one.

- What if she used the wood to build a raft to get the sheep across? But they might get travel sick!

- How about laying stepping stones across the stream? It would take time to train the sheep to use them. But stones might be useful . . .

- She could wade into the stream and support the centre of the wood herself, but she'd risk being swept away. Could something else support it?

28

I'll use the wood to make a bridge and support it by resting it on boulders spaced out across its length. Now it won't bend or break. The boulders will allow the bridge to take the stress of the sheep crossing.

A clapper bridge is a simple bridge, with stone piers for support.

Bridge support

A **bridge** is a **structure** that allows people or vehicles to pass over a river, road or railway. The very first bridges may have been made from tree trunks. Clapper bridges are known to be thousands of years old, and were certainly amongst the first bridges to have been built.

Most bridges have supports underneath that help to carry the weight of the bridge and whatever moves across it. The supports may be made of wood, stone or iron. The support, called a **pier**, acts as a **force** against the **stress** on the bridge. Stress can make the bridge bend out of shape or break.

Stress

Stress is a force or pressure. Stress can make an object change its shape. It can squash or compress something, or it can stretch and expand it. When scientists and engineers talk about calculating stress, they are talking about how to measure the pressure being put on something.

If the stress on an object is too great, the object may bend or even break. A bench, for example, is usually strong enough to resist the stress of people sitting on it. But if you put a big, heavy elephant on the bench, the stress would be too much. The bench would bend and – more likely – break.

A road bridge under construction. Girders are strong enough to bear the stress caused by the weight of the bridge and the traffic crossing it.

STRESSES AND STRAINS

Stress and strain go together. Strain measures how much the shape of an object changes under stress, or how much it bends. The greater the stress, the greater the strain, and the more an object will bend. Rubber, which bends easily, will show greater strain than a tougher material such as steel.

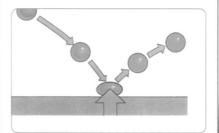

Inventor's words

bridge
compress
expand • force
pier • pressure
strain • stress
structure

Make three different bridges

You will need

- newspaper • glue
- thick cardboard
- paint
- selection of small stones and flat pebbles
- thin card
- wooden cocktail sticks or kebab sticks ·
- string • scissors

1 For the landscape, scrunch up the newspaper to make hills, and glue to the thick cardboard as shown. Between the hills, paste down newspaper scraps to make a smooth surface for the river. Paint the hills and the river.

BEAM BRIDGE

To make a beam bridge, fold a narrow strip of thin card lengthways. Cut small rectangles of card and glue to the bridge to make paving slabs. Glue the bridge to the sides of the hill.

SUSPENSION BRIDGE

To make a suspension bridge, cut up or break cocktail sticks or kebab skewers into 5cm lengths. Tie these on to 2 pieces of string and knot to secure. Tie the ends of the string round large pebbles.

CLAPPER BRIDGE

To make a clapper bridge, place small stones on the river for the piers and flat pebbles for the path across.

DID YOU KNOW?

Clapper bridges are fine for shallow water.
Suspension bridges need strong fixings at each end.
Beam bridges rest on strong girders.

How can we stay dry and safe?

Fenel has decided to give up life as a hunter. He's tired of moving around all the time. He wants to settle down and become a farmer. But he will need a place that will protect him and his wife from the rain and cold, and from wild animals that prowl around.

In the open there is no protection from hungry lions that creep up on people.

He tries standing branches in front of him, but they just fall down.

> How can I shelter and protect myself and my wife from the weather and wild animals?

He must also consider the weather. There are strong winds and rain. Much of the ground will become flooded if the rain continues.

WHAT CAN HE DO?

- Make a pair of stilts and walk around on them. He would be dry and safe from the animals – perhaps . . .

- Build a tree house. But his farm animals would have to stay on the ground.

- Make a round fence of wooden stakes and live behind it. He would still get wet and cold, but it might stop the animals getting in.

- Erecting an umbrella of leaves over the top of the fence might do it. Although the wind would still howl through.

I'll hammer four posts into the ground and make a floor to rest on the posts. Then I'll use four woven fences to make a square building over the raised floor, and put a roof of thatched grass on top. Now I have a shelter that will protect us.

Houses built on stilts are found in places where there is danger of flooding.

Safe shelter

The first **buildings** were simple huts in which families, and sometimes their animals, found **shelter**. The frame of the building was made of interwoven branches, animal tusks or bones. The walls formed a covering, or **cladding**, for the frame. They were probably first made of skins or grasses.

Later buildings were made of wood. Sometimes larger buildings called **longhouses**, single-roomed buildings longer than they were wide, were made to house whole families. In rainy places, some of these homes were built on **stilts**. Houses like these can still be seen in parts of Asia today.

Buildings

A building is a structure with walls and a roof. The walls of the building support each other. They are strong enough to resist outside forces such as wind and rain, and support the roof, which is a heavy load that presses down on the walls.

Modern buildings are made of strong materials that can resist stress from the forces that push against it. These include bricks and mortar – mortar adds great strength to a brick structure. Steel beams, called girders, form a frame around which the walls of the building are fitted. Concrete, a mixture of cement, water and crushed stones, is used to fix the materials together. Piles made of concrete and steel are sunk into holes in the ground to anchor the building.

SWAYING STRUCTURES

Buildings such as skyscrapers have to be strong. But they have to be able to move as well, or they might snap during violent storms. The steel skeleton, or frame, of the building allows it to sway.

Structures such as tall buildings and bridges are constructed with strong materials, including concrete and steel.

Inventor's words

building
cladding
concrete
girder
load • longhouse
mortar
shelter • stilts
structure

Make a house on stilts

You will need

- polystyrene packaging, about 1–2cm thick
- scissors
- thick card from an old carton
- grass, raffia or dried plant stems
- glue • pins
- 4 sticks or straight twigs, about pencil thickness
- thin sticks or wooden skewers
- fine string

1 Use scissors to cut the polystyrene into 2 blocks about 15cm x 10cm. These are the base and roof of the hut. Cut pieces of card for the walls and roof of the hut.

2 Decorate the cards by glueing grass, raffia or dried stems to cover each piece.

PVA

3 Fix the front, back and sides of the hut with pins pushed into the polystyrene blocks. Glue and pin the roof on top.

4 Push the twigs into the base to make the stilts.

5 Make a ladder with the thin sticks and string.

You could make a village with different size huts

How can I paint in colour?

Tribal leader, Awsum, wants a record of his latest victory drawn in colour on the cave walls. Yidah, the tribal artist, argues that he always uses charcoal to make his drawings because he has never made a colour paint that works. But despite Yidah's protests, the leader insists.

He tries to make colours from crushed rocks, but the powder won't stick to the walls.

He makes other colours from crushed flowers, but they're too pale.

Colour would look really good. How can I make colour paints that'll stick to the wall?

He even tries to paint using the blood of an ox mixed with water, but the blood just dries out and the pictures looked cracked and brown.

WHAT CAN HE DO?

- Tell Awsum he is colour blind, so he can still work with charcoal.

- Create battle pictures with whole flower petals. Colourful but not very heroic. And the flowers will soon rot.

- Make colours from crushed rocks and ram's blood, and hope something sticks. Ugh! The crushed rocks have interesting colours, though.

- He really dislikes using blood. Maybe there's another part of the animal that would work.

I know, what if I mixed crushed rock with animal fat? The two substances will make a greasy paste that'll be easy to use and stick to the wall. When it dries out, it will keep its bright colour and thick texture.

A cave painting of a prehistoric fish.

Paste and pigments

Paints are a mixture of dry, coloured powder called a **pigment**, and a sticky substance called a **binder**. When the binder dries out, it fixes the pigment to the surface that is being painted. The first pigments, called earth pigments, came from crushed soft rocks or earth that were coloured by minerals.

Substances such as clay and ochre produced reds, yellows and browns. Charcoal was used to make black. Later, copper oxide was crushed to make green. Mixed together, the pigment and binder produced an oily paint that could be brushed or hand-painted on to a surface.

Fixing paints

Paint is the substance artists use to make a picture. The paint is spread on a surface such as canvas, wood, paper or even stone. Paints are made by mixing dry, powdered colours called pigments with sticky substances called binders. When the sticky binder dries out and hardens, it holds the coloured pigment to the surface.

Modern pigments come from earth that has been coloured by minerals such as iron, or from materials made in a factory. There are many kinds of binders. Some are vegetable gums such as gum arabic, or vegetable oils such as linseed oil. Egg yolks are also used as a binder. Different binders dry out at different speeds, which affect the shine or texture of a painting. Paint can be made thinner by adding a liquid, such as turpentine.

AIRBRUSH

Some modern painters use a special brush to do their work. In fact, it isn't a brush at all but a tiny nozzle that shoots a fine spray of paint on to a surface. A small electric motor powers the machine, which is called an airbrush. An airbrush is often used for technical paintings such as cars.

Inventor's words

binder • canvas
paint • pigment
substance
texture

Today, paint is usually mixed in a big vat.

Make a textured cave painting

You will need

- newspaper
- washing-up bowl
- flour • building brick
- white paint • a paint brush
- natural colouring such as soil, charcoal, crushed berries, ketchup, tomato purée

1 Tear up a sheet of newspaper and place in a bowl of water. Add a spoonful of flour. Leave to soak overnight.

2 Squeeze the pulp, then spread a thin layer on the face of the brick to make a rough texture, like the wall of a cave. Leave to dry.

3 Mix a small amount of white paint as the base, then make different colours using natural ingredients.

4 Use your home-made colours to paint a cave painting on the brick. It will make an attractive bookend or door-stop.

How many colours can you make? What other ingredients did you use?

How can I communicate over a long distance?

Tutenbrodwey loves poetry. As a respected priest, he is allowed to decorate the walls of the temple with his poems. His alphabet is made up of over 2000 symbols known as hieroglyphics. People come from far and wide to read them.

But Tutenbrodwey is not happy. He wants to show his poems to his friends – but they live a long way away.

There is no way to get the temple walls to his friends. And even if they make the long journey to his temple, they will soon forget the poems after they return home.

How can my friends read my poems if they live far away?

WHAT CAN HE DO?

- Copy the poems on to very small clay tablets and send them out with messengers. But he'd need lots of tablets and lots of messengers.

- Write all over a messenger's body and read the poem as he spins round. Giddy work!

- Perhaps he could engrave the poems on something lighter - leaves for example.

- Then he noticed how the local papyrus reed was used in homes to make flat mats. Perhaps he could use flat papyrus for his hieroglyphics.

Papyrus reed will work fine. I'll place strips of it in layers, like a mat. Then I'll press them together to make a thin, flat surface. I could even roll up the papyrus mat and carry it around with me.

An Egyptian priest, or scribe, with a papyrus document.

Papyrus

Papyrus is a water plant that grows in Egypt. It has **reed**-like stems that grow up to 3m high. The ancient Egyptians pressed strips from the stem of the plant between boards. The pressure made the fibres mesh together to create long, rectangular sheets of **porous** white writing material.

These sheets were rolled up into **scrolls** and tied with a leather **thong**, a thin strip of animal hide, or cord. The famous library at Alexandria, Egypt's capital, held over 400,000 papyrus scrolls. They dealt with subjects such as astronomy and geography. Some scrolls lasted for thousands of years.

Picture writing

Imagine what the world was like before writing existed. If people wanted to pass on important information, they had to do so by word of mouth. The listener then had to remember it. Writing allows people to store information: written information can be read by someone in a different place or at a different time.

About 6000 years ago, the people of the ancient Middle Eastern country of Sumer were the first to write down information. They did not use words. Instead, to help remember details of their crops and animals, they scratched pictures called **pictograms** into wet clay. The clay tablets, which were about the size of postcards, became the first kind of stored or portable information, which could be read long after they were written.

PAPER FROM BARK

The kind of paper we know today was invented in China in AD 105. The inventor, Cai Lun, worked in the court of the Chinese Emperor. Cai Lun shred the inner bark of the mulberry tree into fibres. These were then pressed together to make paper. Later, paper was made from rags, rope and even shredded fish nets.

Sumerian pictograms marked on a clay tablet.

Inventor's words

information
paper • papyrus
pictogram
porous
reed
scroll
thong

42

Make your own sheet of paper

Papyrus is made from reeds from the River Nile. You can use a similar method to make paper, using old newspapers.

You will need

- newspaper
- washing-up bowl
- wire mesh • old towels
- big plastic carrier-bag
- board or old tray
- clean kitchen cloth
- scissors • paint

1 Tear up the newspaper into small pieces. Fill a washing-up bowl with water. Add the pieces of paper and leave to soak overnight.

2 Place a piece of fine wire mesh in the kitchen sink and pour a thin layer of newspaper pulp over it.

3 Lift the mesh on to a pile of old towels, cover with a large plastic bag, then press down hard with the board to squeeze out the water.

4 Remove the board, flip the pulp over on to the clean kitchen cloth and carefully remove the wire mesh. Leave to dry out overnight.

5 Remove the paper from the cloth. Trim your paper into a rectangle, and paint with Egyptian hieroglyphics or make a sign for your room.

Use different kinds of waste paper for interesting textures

Glossary and index

Aerodynamic Slippery shape that reduces the effect of friction to allow an object to move more easily through the air.
p.5, 6

Arm Part of a lever that rests on the fulcrum, or pivot.
p.22

Atom Tiniest part of a substance. Atoms are so small that a speck of dust contains a million million atoms.
p.10

Axe Type of wedge with a sharp edge that is attached to a handle. It is used for chopping hard materials such as wood.
p.18

Axle Rod that fits into the hub, or centre, of a wheel.
p.9

Binder Sticky substance that is mixed with pigment to fix paint to a surface.
p.37, 38

Blade Sharp part of a plough that cuts through the soil.
p.17, 18

Bow Wedge-shaped front of a ship.
p.18

Bridge Structure that allows people to pass over a river, valley, road or railway.
p.29

Building Permanent structure in which people can live or work.
p.33, 34

Canvas Strong, coarse cloth that artists use for oil paintings.
p.38

Cladding Protective covering on a material or structure.
p.33

Compress Press or squeeze something to make it smaller.
p.30

Concrete Mixture made up of cement, water and crushed stone that is used for building.
p.34

Crossbeam Horizontal beam made of a strong material that is used to take the weight of a heavy object or building.
p.25

Density Ratio of an object's mass (how much matter there is in an object) to its volume. Density is measured in kilograms per square metre.
p.26

Disc Solid shape that is round, thin and flat.
p.9

Displace Push out of the way. Water can be displaced by a solid object.
p.26

Effort A force. The pull or push force that makes things move or change shape.
p.22

Expand Become bigger or take up more space. Most gases, liquids and solids expand when they are heated.
p.30

Flint Hard rock found as grey or brown pebbles in chalk and limestone.
p.5

Floating To be immersed in water without sinking. An object floats if its weight is less than the weight of the water it displaces.
p.26

Force A push or a pull. Forces make things move or change shape.
p.10, 14, 18, 22, 29, 30, 34

Friction Rubbing of two moving objects against each other, causing them to slow down and produce heat.
p.6, 9, 10

Fulcrum Part of a lever that supports the arm. The rest of the lever pivots or moves around it.   p.22

Furrow Narrow cut or groove in the earth made by a plough, into which seeds are sown.   p.16, 17

Girder Beam made of strong material such as steel that is used to support parts of a structure.   p.34

Gravity Force that pulls objects towards each other. Gravity gives objects weight.
                              p.14

Hieroglyphic Picture writing used by the Ancient Egyptians and other early cultures.   p.40

Inclined plane Sloping surface.   p.14

Inflate Fill with gas or air in order to increase an object's size.   p.25

Information Facts that people learn, or are told or that they hear.   p.4

Irrigate Take water by ditch or other means to dry land when there is not enough rainfall for crops to grow.   p.21

Lever Bar or rod that moves around a fulcrum. The effort of pressing down on one end lifts a load.   p.18, 21, 22

Lintel Horizontal piece of timber or stone across the top of a door or window.   p.12, 13

Load Weight that a force pushes against. Machines move loads while bridges and beams support them.   p.14, 22, 34

Longhouse Single-room building that is longer than it is wide, usually made of wood.   p.33

Megalith Large stone used as part of a prehistoric structure.   p.12, 13

Monument Structure made for a special occasion or religious reason.   p.13

Mortar Mixture of cement, sand and water used to join bricks or stones together, and so strengthen walls.   p.34

Paint Material used for colouring objects.   p.36, 37, 38

Paper Thin material mostly used for writing on or for printing. It can be made from plant fibres or from rags of cotton or linen.   p.42

Papyrus Water plant found on the banks of the River Nile in Egypt. A writing material was made from its stem.   p.40. 41

Pictogram Picture used as a symbol in a system of writing.   p.42

Pier A bridge support that acts on a force against the stress on the bridge.   p.29

Pigment Substance, usually a powder, used to colour paint.   p.37, 38

Plough Machine with a blade that digs into and turns soil ready for seeds to be sown. p.17

Porous Able to absorb air, water or other liquids. p.41

Pressure Amount of force pressing down on the surface of an object. Pressure is measured in newtons per square metre. p.30

Raft Simple boat with a flat bottom and no sides usually powered by a pole, oars or sail. p.25

Ramp Inclined plane, or sloping surface. p.12, 13, 14

Reed Water plant with a long stem. p.41

Scroll Length of writing material rolled around a rod or pair of rods. A scroll is unrolled for reading. p.41

Shadoof Simple machine that raises water based on a lever system. It is often used to irrigate fields. p.21

Shelter Building used for protection from the weather, attack or other phenomena. p.33, 34

Spear Long, aerodynamic pole with a sharp stone or metal blade attached to one end that is used in hunting or warfare. p.5

Stabilise Keep an object firm or fixed so it is not easily moved. p.25

Stilt Long pole used to hold something up or increase its height for protection. p.33

Strain Type of force. A pull that stretches very tightly. p.30

Stress Force that makes an object change its shape. Stress can compress or stretch an object, or make parts of an object slide over each other. p.29, 30, 34

Structure Solid object that encloses, supports or spans other things. p.34

Substance Any kind of matter, whether a solid, liquid or gas. p.26

Texture How a substance or the surface of an object feels to the touch. p.37, 38

Thong Thin strip of leather. p.41

Volume Amount of space an object or liquid takes up. p.26

Wedge Piece of material that is thick at one end and tapers to a sharp edge at the other. As a simple machine, it can change the direction of a force and make it stronger. p.16, 17, 18

Wheel Disc that rotates, or turns, around an axle. p.9

Wind tunnel Building that contains a wind-making machine for testing the aerodynamics of objects such as cars and aeroplanes. p.6

Tools and Materials

Almost all of the materials in this book can be found around the house or bought at your local art or craft shop. If you cannot find the exact item, try and replace it with something similar.

Most of the models will stick fast with PVA glue or even wallpaper paste. However, some materials need a stronger glue, so take care when using these as they may damage your clothes and even your skin. Ask an adult to help you.

Always protect furniture with newspaper or a large cloth, and cover your clothes by wearing an apron.

User Care

Take special care when handling sharp tools such as scissors, pointed gadgets, pieces of wire or craft knives. Ask an adult to help you when you need to use them.